CAMPBELL MORRIS

Advanced Paper Aircraft Construction Mk II

Lions

An Imprint of HarperCollins*Publishers*

Introduction

Welcome to Advanced Paper Aircraft Construction, Mark II *— just when you thought it was safe at last to enter the classroom! Because of the first volume of* Advanced Paper Aircraft Construction, *thousands of happy students, businessmen, handicapped people, politicians, funeral directors, doctors and others are now enjoying their new-found hobby of building paper aircraft. However, if you missed out on all the fun, or you just want to strive for higher technical skill and versatility, this book is for you!*

Although these models are highly advanced, almost anyone can make a superior paper plane by observing the easy-to-follow instructions. Learn how to construct a fantastic Stunt Fly, revolutionary Heliglider and even a Space Shuttle, for those space-hungry venturers.

Almost all the flying devices shown in this book are folded; you don't have to spend endless hours sticking bits of cardboard on as ballast, or cutting here, there and everywhere. All you need is one sheet of paper: an A4 sheet (210 mm x 297 mm) or foolscap is ideal. So now students can rip into their study pads to create instant gliders in any situation.

Paper folding, or origami as it is better known, originated in Japan hundreds of years ago. It had many ceremonial and decorative purposes. Today, it is used to imitate almost anything on this planet and beyond. With paper aircraft, you have the satisfaction of using your creation, rather than just sitting it on the shelf.

So grab a sheet of paper and put your concentration to the test — you'll be more than pleased with the results.

Clubs and Competitions

Clubs are ideal for school students who wish to pool their resources and design new aircraft. These designs can lead to new and even better inventions with paper — all you need is a little imagination! Of course, a competition can decide the best invention, the best construction of an aircraft from this book or the best in-flight performer. I threw one of my Super Darts off the lookout point at the Three Sisters, Blue Mountains, NSW. It took 29 minutes to reach the bottom. A competition for the longest airborne dart or, say, the fastest dart or even the best stunt performer can be held at your school or university.

Types of Paper to Use

All the aircraft in this book use quarto (or A4, 210 x 297 mm) or foolscap paper. Make sure you use thin but strong paper. Never use anything like newspaper, which is not strongly bonded and therefore cannot hold a fold. If the paper is too heavy, it might inhibit the more complicated folds shown in this book.

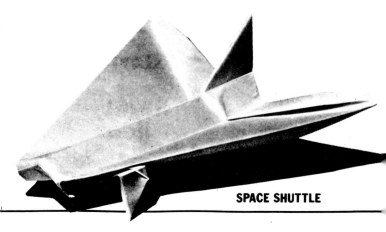

SPACE SHUTTLE

Explanation of Symbols

The symbols are very important if you are to succeed when folding. The following symbols will be used throughout this book. Before you start folding your first winner, a little practice with small pieces of paper will help.

Larger view of previous diagram.

Smaller view of previous diagram.

When this valley fold has a dotted line it means that the rest of the fold is hidden under a flap etcetera.

Fold in general direction of arrow.

Turn the model over.

Push in.

Sectional view — only that part of the diagram necessary for the fold is shown.

Crease-fold — fold in direction of arrow, then unfold.

Detailed view to be shown.

Stair-step fold.

Cut along dotted line.

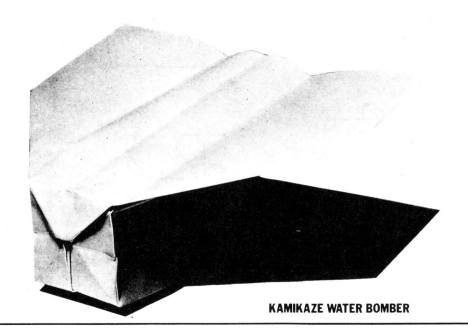

KAMIKAZE WATER BOMBER

Folding Techniques

Getting the fold right is only half the job. The real skill is in throwing the completed dart. As you will discover, each aircraft requires a special throwing technique.

Finally, take it slowly, fold accurately and throw with precision — it's bound to provoke a reaction from fellow students and friends!

1

Valley fold (indicated by a line of dashes) — fold in direction of arrow along the line of dashes.

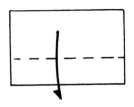

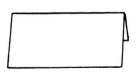

2

Mountain fold (indicated by a line of dots and dashes) — fold in direction of arrow BEHIND YOU along the line of dots and dashes.

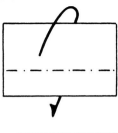

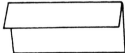

3

Reverse fold — crease along the dotted line and fold outwards as shown.

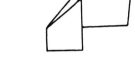

4

Inverse fold — crease along the dotted line and push inwards as shown.

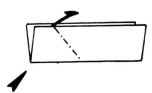

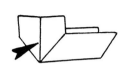

5

"Rabbit ear" fold — make creases and then fold the two sides inwards, bringing them to touch the bottom line and forming a point or "ear".

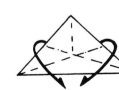

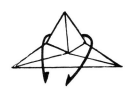

(top and side view)

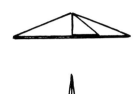

Paper Plane Base Folds

Later in this book you will come across more complicated aircraft that start with one of these base folds. It is essential that you learn them first before embarking on the more complicated models. These base folds are also the foundation for making new and even more complicated designs of your own. A little practice and imagination can go a long way!

Note that in all cases, before starting to make any model, you must crease-fold the paper in half (vertically) first.

Paper Plane Base Fold No. 1

This is the simplest of the base folds. When doing the mountain fold, it is easiest to turn the paper over (the mountain fold becomes a valley fold), then turn the paper back over and push your finger into the point where all the creases meet. The sides should pop up making it easy to complete the base fold.

1.
Fold and crease the valley folds AD and BC, then the mountain fold EF.

2.
Move the sides inwards, bringing the top edge downwards.

3.
The completed fold.

Paper Plane Base Fold No. 2

1.
Fold down the top corners first as in a normal dart.
Then unfold them and fold the top edges down to meet the creases thus left.

2.
With B as the axis bring point A down to align with side BD as shown and crease. Repeat on the other side with C as the axis. Mountain fold where shown.

3.
Bring in top and sides.

4.
The completed base fold.

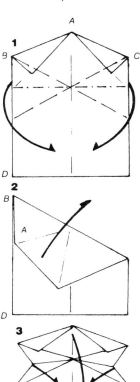

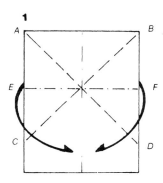

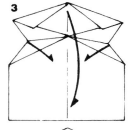

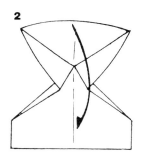

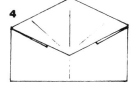

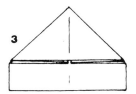

Air Hopper

A graceful glider that will "flap" its wings and hop through the air like a butterfly.

1.

Use a sheet of A4 or foolscap paper. Remember that in most cases you should fold it in half first to make a crease. In this case, have the paper horizontally facing you. Fold the top corners down.

2.

Fold the top point down to meet the bottom edge.

3.

Tuck your finger under point A, bringing point B over to the centre crease, noting valley and mountain folds involved.

4.

Halfway there. Do the same for the other side.

5.

Fold the centre point up, then mountain fold in half.

6.

Fold wings down in both positions indicated. If you want a straight (non-stalling) glider fold down along only one of the lines indicated to determine stability (see asterisk).

7.

The completed Air Hopper.

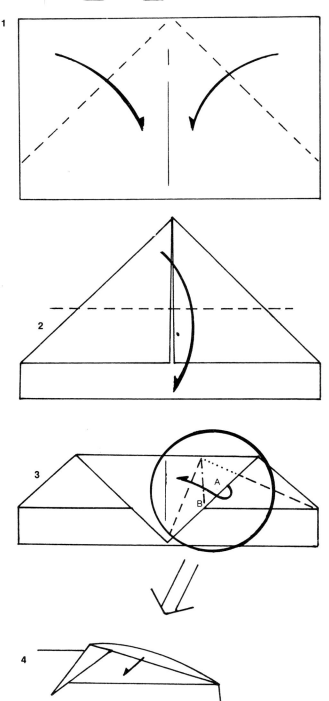

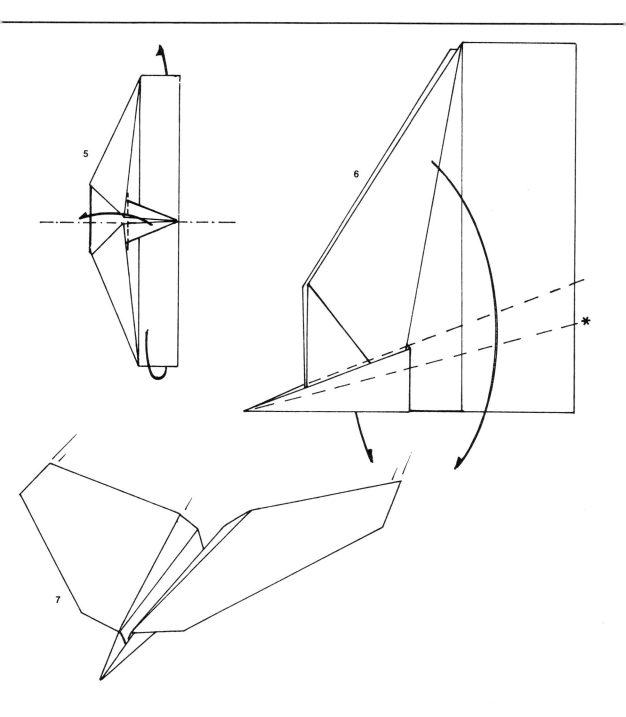

Throwing Suggestions

For loops — using heavier and more rigid paper, throw hard and high into the air.

Alternatively, you can let it glide from a high spot, say, from the back row of an opera house, and it will hop up and down, annoyingly distracting the conductor and everyone else.

Stunt Fly

This beast can be either a menace to fellow students, or a graceful glider, flying over to perch on your shoulder or someone's mortar-board!

1.
Use A4 paper only (or shorten a piece of foolscap). Fold in half upwards.

2.
Valley fold in the general area indicated.

3.
Place your finger under A, bringing the flap over to the right. Note the hidden section of the valley fold.

4.
Fold end several times (approximately eight or nine times depending on weight distribution factor).

5.
Fold in half.

6.
Bring wings down. Note hidden fold detail. Make a small "rabbit-ear" kink in the forward section so that the centre tail can remain upright.

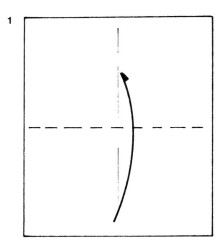

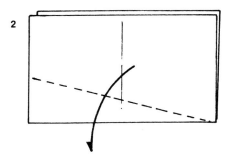

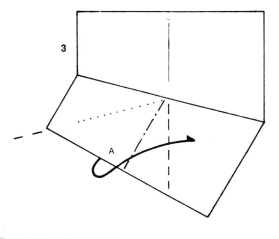

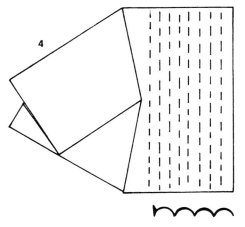

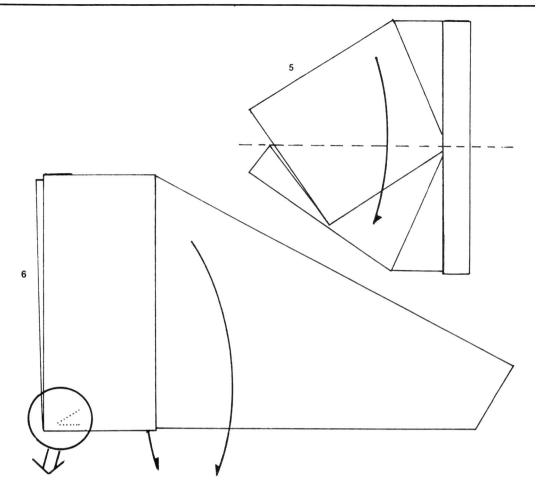

Throwing Suggestions

Make sure your model is perfectly symmetrical. To make it return to you in a vertical circle, grasp the centre-forward section with the underside facing you. Lift it up and away from you. It should loop. To make a horizontal circle with underside facing you, throw upwards at a 30-degree angle away from you. This is quite a versatile creature that will have nature lovers intrigued by its graceful manoeuvrability. If it lands on your desk — don't swat it!

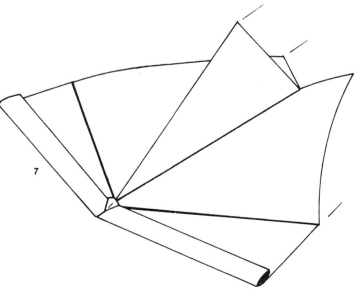

7.
The completed Stunt Fly.

Elasto-Kinetic Jet
(sling shooter)

You're sitting calmly in the examination room. Mathematical figures are flying through your mind as you try to solve the equation before the exam ends. Suddenly white lightning soars past you, striking the examiner right between the eyes! Lightning? No! It was that fat jerk sitting behind you with his Elasto-Kinetic Jet.

You don't need to be a maths genius to make this dart!

1.
Crease and unfold the corners on your foolscap sheet of paper.

2.
Fold corners so that they meet the original crease.

3.
Fold the new edges in so that they meet the centre crease.

4.
Fold once again to meet the centre crease.

5.
Fold point to meet side edge.

6.
Fold edge twice for weight factor. Then mountain fold in half.

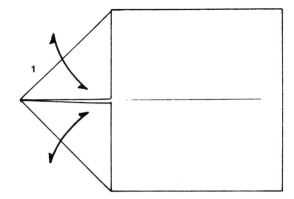

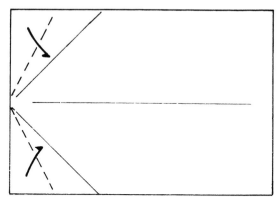

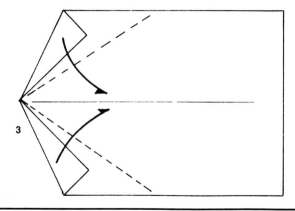

7.
Note point A. This ensures that the centre fuselage is tough enough to withstand stress upon launching. Next cut out small section where indicated and fold down wings. You may wish to add side flaps for more stability. Curl up wings for lift if necessary.

8.
The completed Elasto-Kinetic Jet.

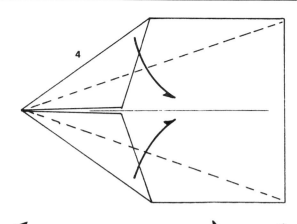

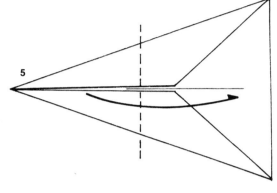

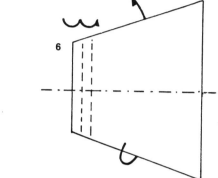

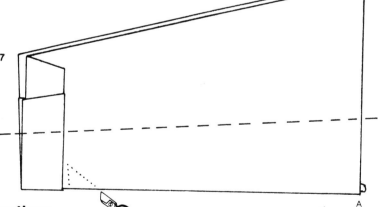

Throwing Suggestions
Hook an average-size rubber band in the cut-out section and with your fingers grasp section A (shown in diagram 7). Stretch back and let go. If you add more lift at the rear tail section and aim high, you can do an exceptionally fast loop . . . just like Buck Rogers!

(**NOTE:** Works best when drawn back across your arm, using the arm as a "launching strip".)

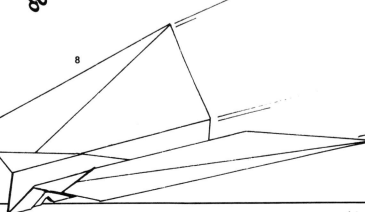

Stingray Glider

When I threw one of these at work one day, it became stuck at the top of a door. It happened to be the door to a management conference. As the boss opened the door the glider flew off and landed on the main desk. I wonder what the management think their employees do all day!

1.
Fold corners on your sheet of foolscap or A4 paper.

2.
Fold edges in to meet centre crease.

3.
Stair-step fold where indicated.

4.
Place finger inside point A and bring edge across to meet centre crease (see Air Hopper for similar fold).

5.
Almost there. Do the same for the other side.

6.
Now mountain fold in half.

7.
Fold wings down.

8.
The completed Stingray Glider. Add tail lift by curling up wings if necessary.

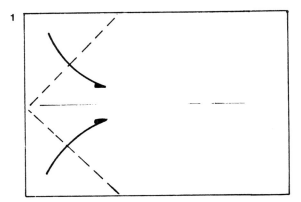

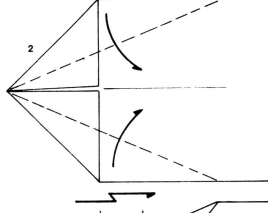

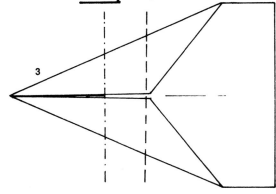

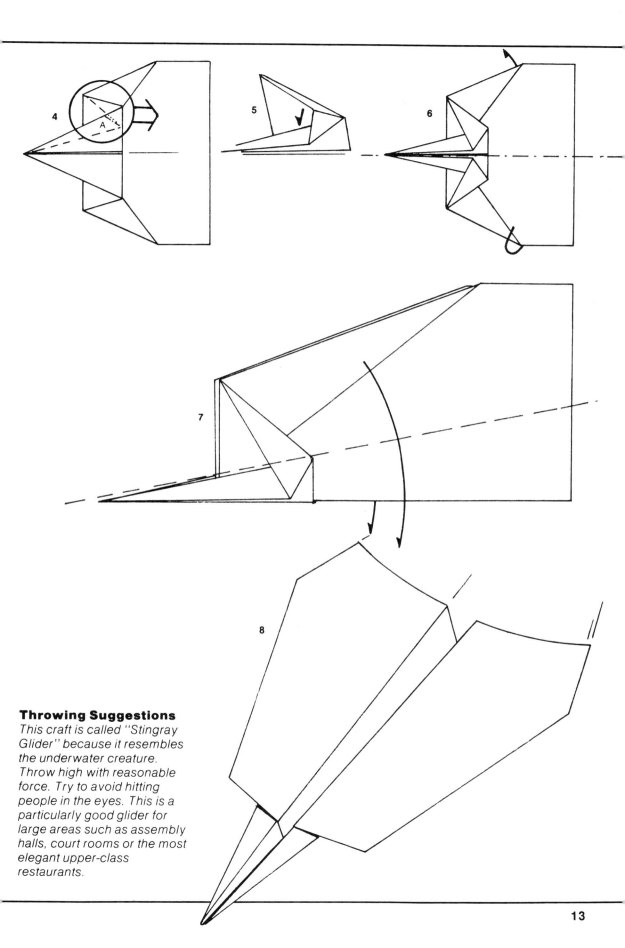

Throwing Suggestions

This craft is called "Stingray Glider" because it resembles the underwater creature. Throw high with reasonable force. Try to avoid hitting people in the eyes. This is a particularly good glider for large areas such as assembly halls, court rooms or the most elegant upper-class restaurants.

Winged-Keel Glider

(controversial)

A controversial design that will win the hearts of many if ever someone comes up with an America's Cup Air Race (maybe it could compete with a Perth Plate used as a frisbee)! This is an original one-piece-of-paper design that can catch those high sea breezes and make a winner of anyone who folds it.

1.
Fold corners on your sheet of foolscap paper.

2.
Fold edges in to meet centre crease.

3.
Stair-step fold where indicated.

4.
Make a big "rabbit-ear".

5.
Detailed diagram of the completed "rabbit-ear".

6.
Fold the section once or twice for weight distribution factor. Then mountain fold in half.

7.
Keel section. Make a "rabbit-ear" fold, bringing point A upwards and parallel to the hull . . . er . . . fuselage of the craft, Add side flaps and tail flaps for stability and lift.

8.
The completed Winged-Keel Glider.

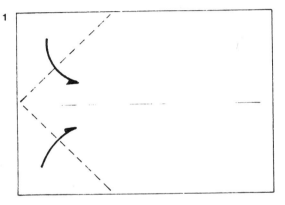

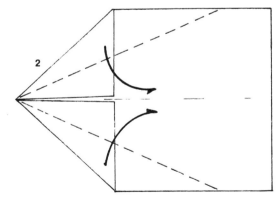

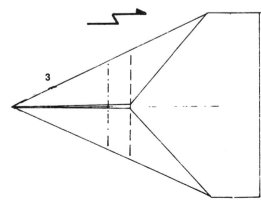

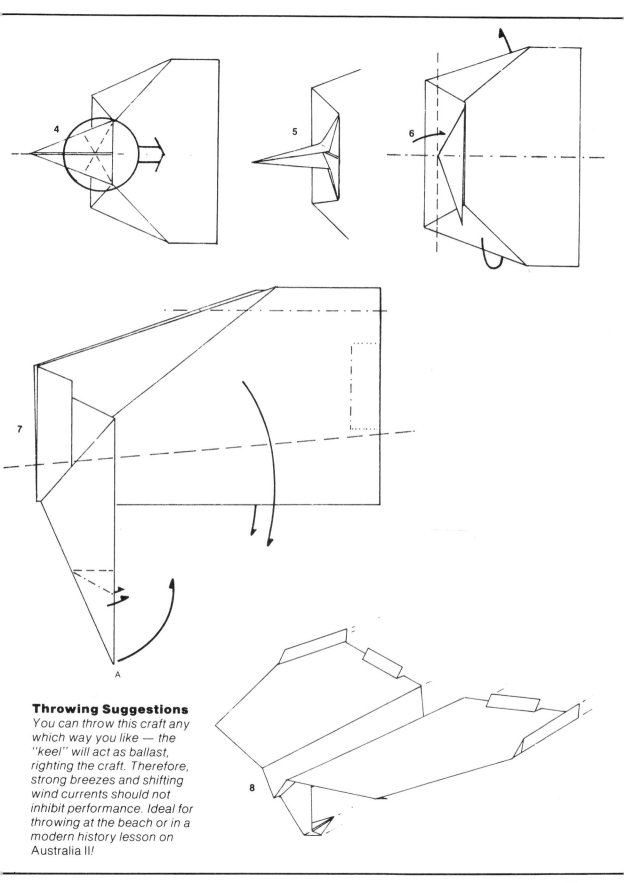

Throwing Suggestions

You can throw this craft any which way you like — the "keel" will act as ballast, righting the craft. Therefore, strong breezes and shifting wind currents should not inhibit performance. Ideal for throwing at the beach or in a modern history lesson on Australia II!

UFO

I call this model a UFO simply because I don't know what else to call it! Perhaps it could be something out of Star Trek? Often the weirdest-looking craft can perform outstandingly well and this model is no exception.

1.
Use a sheet of foolscap or A4 paper horizontally facing you. Make a centre crease and then fold the top end down five to seven times at approximately 8 mm width each time. You may change these specifications depending on required weight and lift.

2.
Fold in half.

3.
At approximately one-third of the distance from left to right, cut along dotted line and fold flap across, making sure point A meets edge (point B). Do the same on the other side.

4.
Add side flaps and tail flaps and fold wings down. Now for the tricky bit: forward wings must be locked together.

5.
Detailed view. Open up point C and slide in section D-E (hidden fold). It should tuck in nicely and hold the forward section firmly.

6.
The completed UFO.

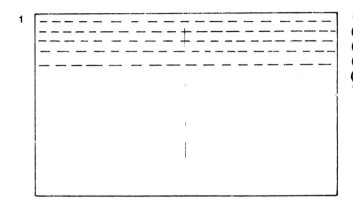

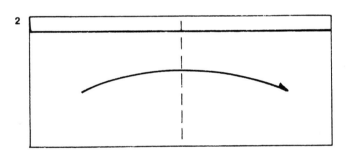

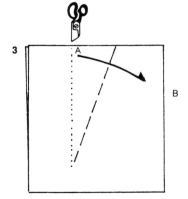

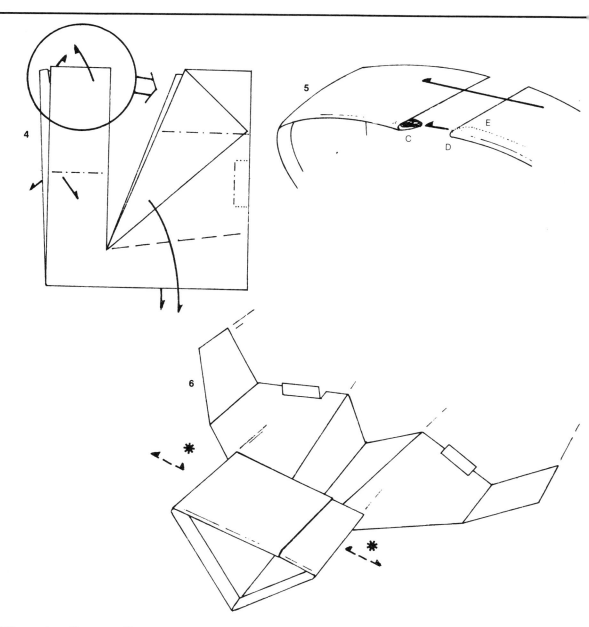

Throwing Suggestions

The wing section can be widened or shortened depending on the stability and angle of descent you require (see asterisks on diagram 6). A versatile craft indeed.

Place your forefinger inside the tail section of the fuselage, with your thumb underneath the tail section. Let your craft go on a slight downward grade. If symmetry is good, it will glide magnificently to meet a straight target . . . perhaps a teacher?

Starfighter

This is the perfect craft for those who love science fiction! Imagine throwing one of these in the cinema while Return of the Jedi is showing. The audience will like the movie, but they'll just love the live-action scene when your Starfighter streaks down the aisle!

1.
Begin with a foolscap sheet horizontally facing you. Fold the bottom corners up and behind.

2.
Fold the top edge over six times at approximately 1 cm intervals.

3.
Fold A across to meet centre crease along valley fold B. Do the same for D and C. Make centre folds where indicated to form fuselage.

4.
With model turned over and the underside facing you, feed point E inside point F. Continue to push inwards for about 3 cm.

5.
Larger sectional view. This is how it should look. Now make a crease fold in the centre and bring in the sides of the craft as shown in the finished plane (diagram 6).

6.
The completed Starfighter. Lengthen or shorten wingspan to determine best performance (see UFO).

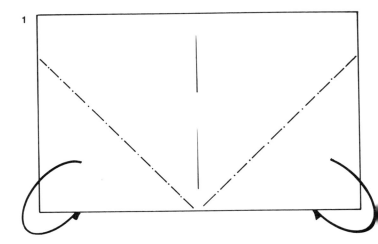

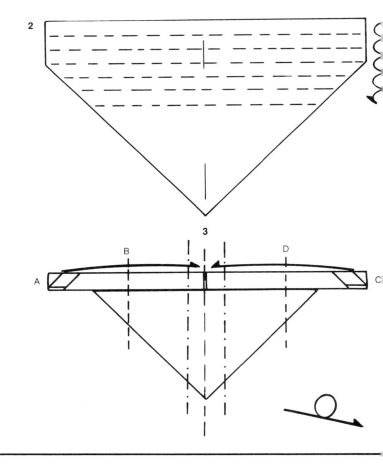

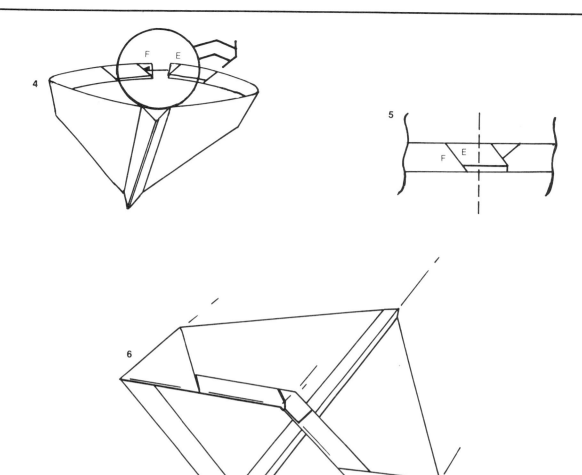

4

5

F E

6

Throwing Suggestions

Hold the fuselage with finger and thumb and throw high with moderate force. It may loop if you so desire, or glide magnificently when thrown gently. Perhaps Steven Spielberg could use this design in his next Hollywood set?

Stunt Glider

A good outdoor craft that can glide-circle, do loops and handle strong breezes without being toppled. It resembles a flying arrow — something that will stand out from the usual paper glider.

1.
Crease fold where indicated, then fold the sides inwards as if you were making a base fold. A heavier foolscap sheet is preferable.

2.
Almost there.

3.
Fold top point down, tucking the two side flaps inside the top flap.

4.
Almost there.

5.
Fold in half.

6.
Fold down wings and add side flaps.

7.
The completed Stunt Glider.

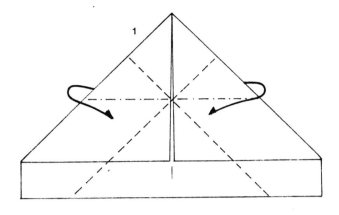

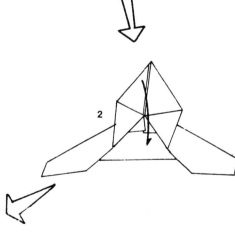

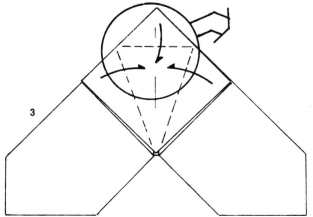

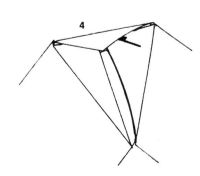

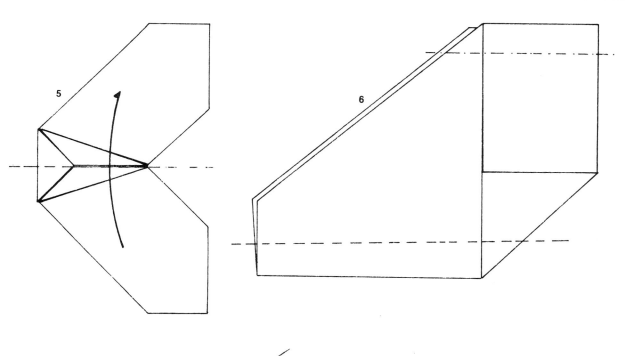

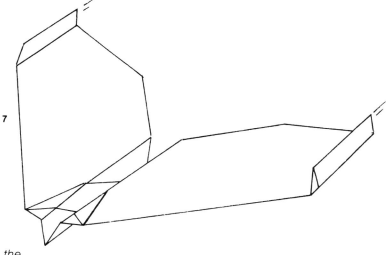

Throwing Suggestions

Throw hard and high into the air and against the wind. Depending on wind strengths it should loop or catch an upper air current and glide away. With the underside facing you, you can throw upwards at a 30-degree angle to make it circle. Don't forget — practice makes perfect!

*(**NOTE:** Birds seem to love this particular design. I threw mine high one day and a kookaburra swooped down to investigate, following its glide path.)*

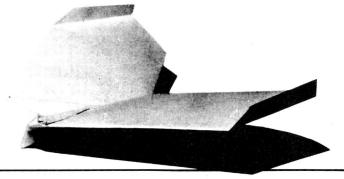

Runway Skimmer

An amazing glider with a folded undercarriage that ensures a somewhat interesting landing upon a teacher's desk. As it lands upon a smooth surface it skims and flies even further!

1.
Begin with a sheet of A4 and fold Paper Plane Base Fold No. 1. Fold top flap up where indicated, noting centre fold.

2.
Almost complete.

3.
Fold top end behind.

4.
Mountain fold in half.

5.
Fold down wings, undercarriage and feet. Add lift to tail section if necessary. For more direction, add side flaps.

6.
The completed Runway Skimmer.

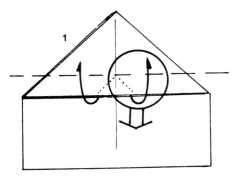

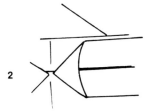

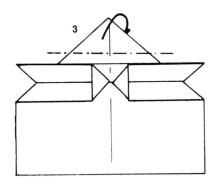

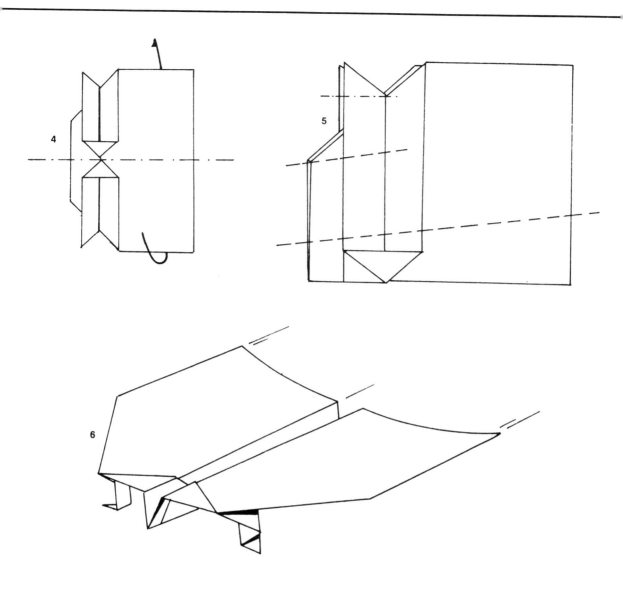

Throwing Suggestions

Let go gently in a downward motion. If it lands on a smooth surface, say, a headmaster's desk or the manager's desk (which would be much longer) the spring action on the undercarriage will "bounce" the craft up; and probably over the edge.

Dart Attack

The war is on! Paper darts are flying everywhere, throughout the lecture hall, as the students demonstrate what they think of the lecturer! Now imagine you had the ultimate in paper fighting "machines" — something with gun turrets or landing gear that would annoyingly stick in someone's hair. The fighter of your imagination is only as far away as the piece of paper in front of you!

1.
Begin with Paper Plane Base Fold No. 1. Make a "rabbit-ear" on the top right-hand flap.

2.
Almost there. Do the same for the other side.

3.
Open out the "rabbit-ear" by tucking your finger inside and folding where indicated.

4.
Fold top half down, then fold across to the right. Do the same for the other side.

5.
Fold the two sides inwards.

6.
Mountain fold in half.

7.
Reverse fold the "feet" or guns where indicated and open outwards. Cut where indicated on tail fuselage, then inverse fold to make a fin. Fold down wings and side flaps where indicated.

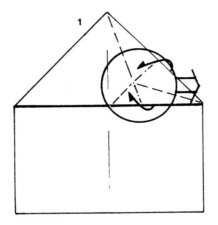

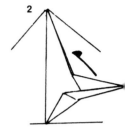

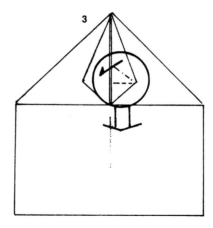

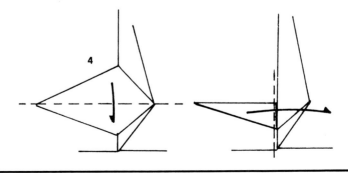

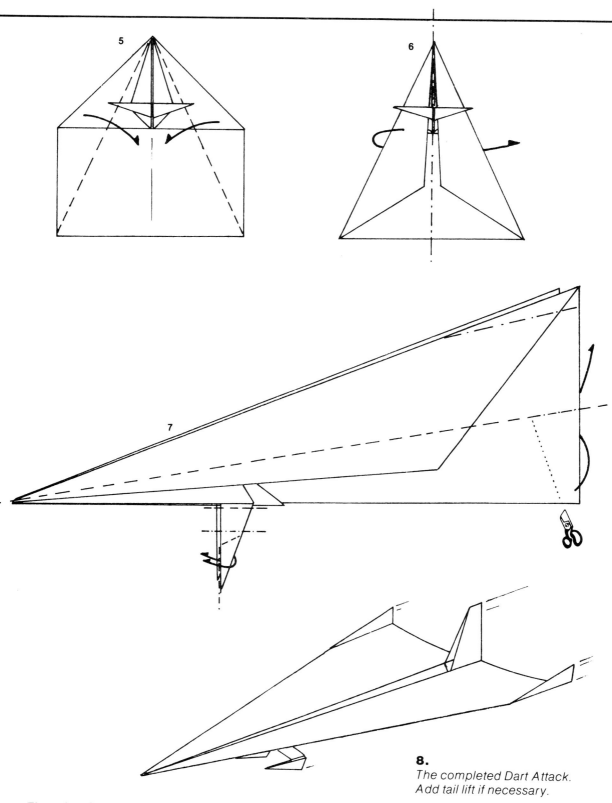

8.
The completed Dart Attack.
Add tail lift if necessary.

Throwing Suggestions
Throw hard and high, aiming
for anything that dares to take
you on!

Dive Bomber

Just like Buck Rogers! This craft will make a huge swooping dive, picking up momentum and gathering lift. The model forward guns add a more realistic effect.

1.
Begin with Paper Plane Base Fold No. 2. Foolscap or A4 paper is ideal. Note your base fold points A and B. Run a vertical valley fold up from these points and then make a fold similar to a "rabbit-ear" by tucking your finger inside the top flap and folding where indicated.

2.
Almost there.

3.
Once this fold is done on both sides, you can lift the flap (point C) upwards and fold where indicated.

4.
Almost there.

5.
Turn model over.

6.
Valley fold where indicated.

7.
Valley fold top section down where indicated. The two points behind should flip up.

8.
Now mountain fold in half.

9.
Mountain and valley fold wings where indicated.

10.
The completed Dive Bomber.

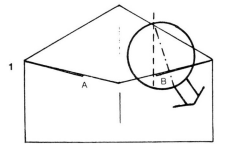

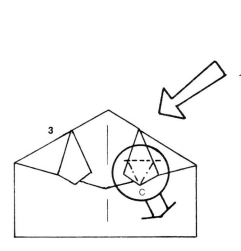

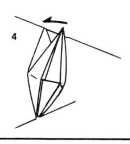

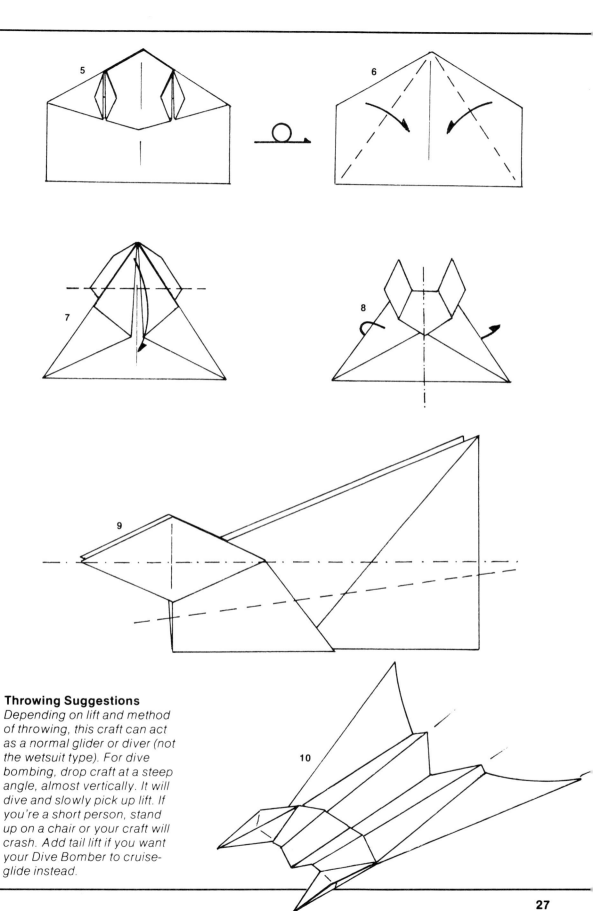

Throwing Suggestions

Depending on lift and method of throwing, this craft can act as a normal glider or diver (not the wetsuit type). For dive bombing, drop craft at a steep angle, almost vertically. It will dive and slowly pick up lift. If you're a short person, stand up on a chair or your craft will crash. Add tail lift if you want your Dive Bomber to cruise-glide instead.

Heliglider

You'd freak if you saw this hovering in the school assembly area! That's because this craft is a technological masterpiece representing a combination of helicopter and glider; yet it is surprisingly simple. Folded correctly, it will prove a unique talking piece for physics students and others.

1.
Begin with a foolscap sheet of paper. Cut an approximately 2 cm strip off the tail end, but don't throw it out! Fold top corners in.

2.
Fold sides in.

3.
Fold top point down to meet bottom edge.

4.
Folding where indicated, edge A must meet the centre crease. When this is established points C and B will fold across.

5.
Like so — almost there.

6.
Fold top end down two or three times depending on the weight you wish to achieve. Then fold in half.

7.
Note hidden folds. Inverse fold the centre point upwards. This is the centre "propeller" shaft. On final folding, you must work out balance. It is critical in the performance of your craft. Therefore, the centre shaft can be folded from a more forward of aft position.

8.
What it should look like. Fold the wing across and leave aside for the moment.

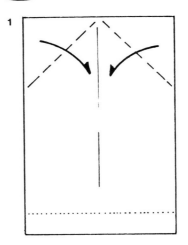

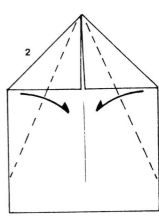

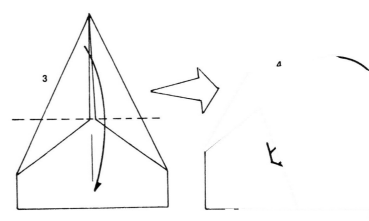

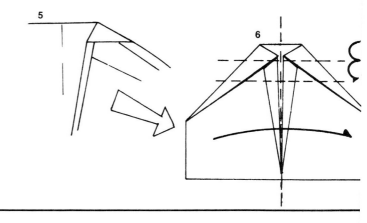

9.

Now, remember the paper strip? If it hasn't wound up in the backyard barbecue, grab it and fold in half as shown in diagram 9. Fold where indicated at opposite angles leaving some vertical headroom at the top.

10.

It should look something like this.

11.

Fold down wings on your glider section where indicated.

12.

Now grab a pin from the nearest tax form or sewing box. Make sure it's an average everyday type about 1 ½ cm long with a head on it. Feed the pin through the centre of your rotor blade (note the two dots) two or three times to secure it together. Then feed it through the top of the shaft two or three times making sure the rotor can rotate smoothly. Add side flaps to the craft for more stability if you wish. Slight tail lift if necessary.

13.

The completed Heliglider.

Throwing Suggestions

Throw gently away from you in a slight downward motion with the rotor blades facing horizontally towards you. For better performance, give the rotor blades a slight curl upwards as shown in diagram 12. This will reinforce the blade, preventing it being "floppy". Also note that the centre of the rotor blade must be kept secured by the pin.

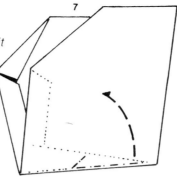

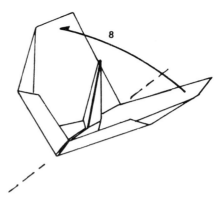

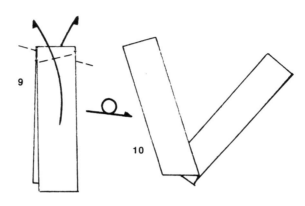

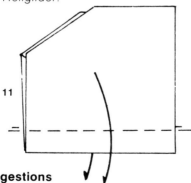

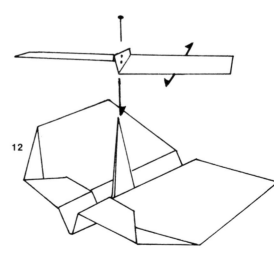

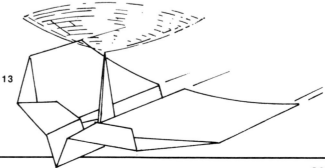

Space Shuttle

Now here is an inexpensive way to build and fly your space shuttle without spending a fortune on silicone matting or having to replace the occasional missing tile!

1.
Make a slight crease fold in the centre of a sheet of foolscap paper. Now fold the bottom side in to make another crease fold. Tear or cut off the strip of paper, making the foolscap sheet proportionately longer.

2.
Make a new centre crease and fold Paper Plane Base Fold No. 1 as shown. Fold the left hand corners then fold right hand sides in as shown — under the top flap.

3.
Stair-step fold where indicated and make a "rabbit-ear" on the other end of the craft.

4.
How it should look. Detailed fold shown.

5.
Fold flap, flattening point A.

6.
The asterisk indicates how the undercarriage is folded upon completion of your craft. You may wish to use your own ingenuity to make the undercarriage more complicated.

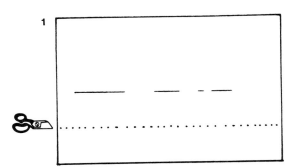

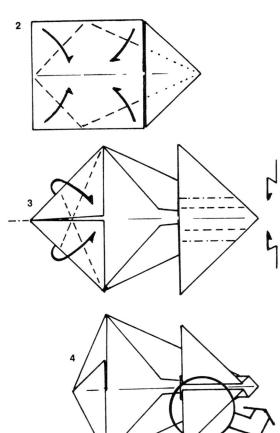

7.
*Fold end two or three times
depending on correct weight
needed for flight. Then fold the
left side "rabbit-ear" behind.
After you have done this,
valley fold in half.*

8.
*Fold wings up at a slight angle
and then fold the
undercarriage as shown in
diagram 6.*

9.
*The completed Space Shuttle.
Tail lift should not be
necessary, though extra
weight may be needed if your
craft stalls. Try inversing the
forward nose section at an
angle or adjust undercarriage
to reduce drag.*

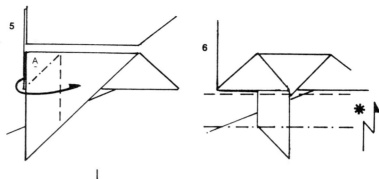

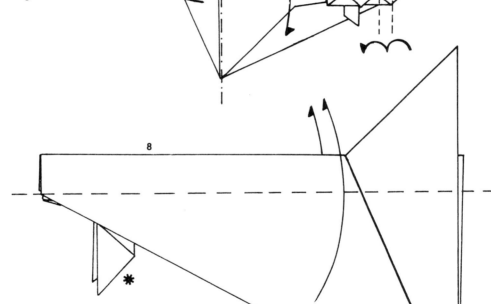

Throwing Suggestions
*Have your craft at a slight
downward angle, holding the
tail fin with your finger and
thumb. With slight motion, let it
drop — it will glide to a smooth
touchdown.*
  *Ideal for lecture halls if the
discussion is on space
technology!*

Kamikaze Water Bomber

Wow! A flying projectile (you can use it only once, hence "Kamikaze") that will have umpires storming off the cricket ground or politicians crossing the floor.

1.
Begin with a foolscap sheet but take approximately 3 cm off the side of the sheet to make it proportionately longer. See diagram 1 p.30.

2.
Fold Paper Plane Base Fold No. 1. Fold the flaps in.

3.
Fold flaps where indicated.

4.
Tuck point A inside the pocket B as shown in direction of arrow.

5.
Like so.

6.
Once you've made this fold to the other side, fold the whole flap behind.

7.
With the model turned over, inverse fold corners.

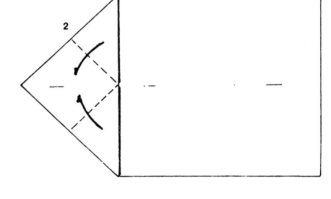

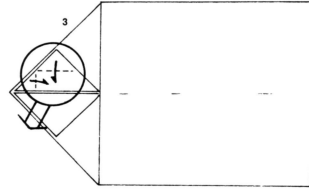

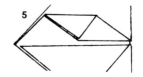